ST OLAV OF NORWAY

ST OLAV OF NORWAY
KING, SAINT — AND ENIGMA

BY

Vera Henriksen

ISBN 82-518-2055-3
Engers Boktrykkeri A/S, Otta

Contents

Once upon a Time

To most Norwegians the story of Olav the Saint is a delightful fairy tale. He is the good king who pitted Christian justice against Viking cruelty, the king who brought Norsemen from dark ignorance into the bosom of European civilization. He is the martyr who, in the year 1030 on July 29th — at the battle of Stiklestad where his army of Christians fought against a pagan host — gave his life for his faith. He is the Saint whose miracles before and after his death converted his country.

But looking into the source material, the history of our Saint becomes considerably more complex. Actually, one is met with what in modern terms could be called a split personality — split, indeed, in no less than five different ways.

There is the brutal Viking, the humble and pious Saint of the Church, the pagan descendant of gods, a man who was also considered the reincarnation of a former king — and there is Olav Haraldsson, hero of the most famous of the sagas, the one recorded by the Icelandic historian Snorri Sturluson during the period A.D. 1225—1230. Finally, there is the king Olav of folklore — the vanquisher of trolls and giants, a magic figure who made any number of healing springs gush forth, and who even left his footprints in hard rock.

In the telling of this, at times, amazing tale, I shall do what may be considered unorthodox: step out of the traditional and impersonal role of the author, to be a personal guide to the sources that relate the story of our many-faceted Saint.

I do not guarantee that we shall find true answers to the many riddles of his life. But, nevertheless, I believe that ours will be a worthwhile excursion into the world of ancient poems, chronicles, sagas, legends — and fairy tales.

St Olav treading on a human figure, generally thought to represent his enemies. This wooden statue from the latter part of the 13th century (Tanum Church, Brunlanes, Vestfold) is characteristic of the Saint-Olav-statues of that period. Another attribute of the Saint is an ax, supposed to be the weapon by which he was martyred, usually carried in his right hand.

Within a Framework of History

The unsolved riddles of Saint Olav do not concern the historical outline of his life — on that topic modern historians are in general agreement.

I shall list the main events for reference:

Born approximately A.D. 990, possibly somewhat later, Olav Haraldsson (i.e. the son of Harald) claimed to be a descendant of Harald Hårfagre ('Fairhair'), the first king to gather under his rule much of present-day Norway. According to the most notable estimate of historians, Harald Hårfagre died in the year 932 or 933.

Very young — according to the sagas at the age of twelve, and under the guardianship of his foster father — Olav Haraldsson chose the life of a Viking chieftain. He found himself a ship and crew and set out to plunder and kill — entirely in the tradition that made him and his likes the dread of Christian Europe.

In the year 1013, or thereabouts, he was converted to Christianity. His baptism probably took place at Rouen in France.

The following year he returned to Norway (from England) to claim the inheritance from Harald Hårfagre. In a decisive sea-battle that took place on Palm Sunday 1016, he vanquished his most important rival, earl Svein of the Lade clan. Lade is an estate now situated within the limits of the city of Trondheim. Since the earls of Lade — Svein, his brother Eirik and his nephew Håkon — had ruled Norway as vassals to the Danish and Swedish kings, his good fortune brought Olav the enmity of his neighbours to the east and south. Unfortunately the king of Denmark at the time was the powerful Knut (Canute the Great), ruler also of England.

Some eightyfive years ago the sagas of the Norwegian kings, as written by the Icelandic historian Snorri Sturluson around the year 1230, were published in an edition illustrated by a group of renowned artists. Since then this illustrated version has been published several times, and Snorri's narrative is inseparably linked to those illustrations in the minds of most Norwegians – even though the pictures may leave a bit to be desired as far as the historical accuracy of clothing and other details is concerned.

    Here is an artist's conception of king Olav preparing for the very important battle of Nesjar, on Palm Sunday of the year 1016.

Olav Haraldsson's reign, which lasted from the year 1016 till just before Christmas of the year 1028, was overshadowed by the consequences of that battle.

During the first couple of years, until around 1019, he conducted a struggle with the Swedish king. But eventually they settled for peace, and Olav Haraldsson married a daughter of his Swedish colleague.

However, a good many of Norway's leading chieftains had close ties with the Lade family, and were consequently reluctant to give Olav their loyalty. — The word chieftain, as used here, needs an explanation. Norway possessed no formal nobility at the time, and 'chieftains' rather designate those untitled men of power who represented leading families and were tied to each other by bonds of kinship and common interests. —

Given the choice between submission and exile or death, the majority of these men chose to submit, but they did so without enthusiasm.

Furthermore, Olav's reign was remarkable for his missionary zeal. He brought priests and bishops from England and demanded conversion from all his subjects. Those who resisted, were threatened with mutilation and/or the confiscation or burning of their property. This undoubtedly made him unpopular with the peasants, many of whom were attached to their pagan gods and not minded to abandon them. He also forced people to accept laws which made Christianity mandatory, including such Christian practices as fasting on Fridays and doing a minimum of work on Sundays. But neither his faith nor his Christian laws seem to provide the ultimate reason why the chieftains eventually rebelled — their main objection to king Olav was, more probably, the king's centralization of power in his own hand.

Meanwhile king Knut of England and Denmark bided his time. Not until the middle of the 1020'ies did he decide to settle his accounts with king Olav. At that stage most of the Norwegian chieftains had had more than enough of Olav Haraldsson, and were ready to join Knut in the effort to drive Olav from the country. When Knut came to Norway with a huge fleet in the year 1028, he did not fight a single battle. He was proclaimed

This stone cross with its runic inscription is thought to be contemporary with king Olav Haraldsson. The inscription is interpreted thus: ' ... the priest put up this stone in memory of Erling, his lord ... when he fought Olav.'

The priest's name is illegible. But Erling was the name of a powerful chieftain of southwestern Norway, who rebelled against king Olav, was taken prisoner by him and killed by one of the king's men in the year 1028. According to the sagas the king then uttered: 'By that blow you struck Norway out of my hand.' Erling had been popular as well as powerful – alive he might have saved the tottering regime of king Olav; his death, however, signalled the final stage of the general rebellion that drove the king into exile.

king of Norway in one district after another, and Olav was driven into exile by his own countrymen.

King Olav spent his exile, lasting little more than a year and a half, partly in Sweden, partly in Russia where his wife's half-sister was married to the grand duke, ruler of the Russian state of which Kiev was the capital.

As for king Knut, he reinstated earl Håkon of Lade as his vassal ruler of Norway.

When word reached Kiev some time during the winter of the years 1029—1030 that earl Håkon had drowned, Olav decided that the time was ripe for an attempt at reconquering his lost kingdom.

He returned to Norway via Sweden the following spring. On the way he gradually collected an army consisting in part of Swedish mercenaries which the king of Sweden had allowed him to recruit — he also assembled groups of Norwegians who had remained true to him and come to Sweden to join him, and a few adventurers who felt inclined to try their fortune.

With this more or less ragtag army, he went into battle at Stiklestad on the 29th of July — and was beaten by an army of Norwegians loyal to king Knut. In this connection it should be pointed out that Knut, too, was a Christian king, and that there were Christians as well as pagans in the army fighting against king Olav at Stiklestad. It was never a question of Olav and his noble Christians fighting a pagan horde. It is even doubtful whether Olav's army was made up exclusively of Christians — a point to which we shall return.

King Olav died in that battle.

And a year later bishop Grimkjell, an Anglo-Saxon who had come with Olav to Norway in the year 1015 and had followed him on most of his journeys to various parts of the country as his loyal friend, canonized the king. At that time such a procedure was proper and valid; the right to canonize had not yet been reserved the Papal See.

King Olav left two children, a daughter born to his queen, Astrid, and a son born out of wedlock — the boy's mother was one of the queen's servingwomen.

But, although we know a great deal about king Olav, there remain several open questions.

One of them concerns bishop Grimkjell's decision. Why did he canonize Olav Haraldsson? Was he of the opinion that the king had lived a pious life in true Christian humility and had died for his faith? Or did he have other reasons, reasons that may have been related to Church policy — for instance, the conviction that in order to obtain a genuine conversion of the Norsemen of the time, the canonization of a royal saint was needed?

Other questions concern the king himself.

How truly converted was he? Did he genuinely regard himself as the instrument of Christ, or did he, on the contrary, avail himself of Christ as a means of manifesting his own power over men? Was he a truly pious man, or was he simply a brutal Viking in Christian guise?

These are the questions to be borne in mind when consulting the sources.

As a further aid to readers unfamiliar with Norwegian history, a short summary of king Olav's life will be given (p. 77).

Those who told the Story

This section is not intended to be a list of sources and literature
— those interested in such a list, will find one at the end of this
book — . Rather, my aim has been that of providing a general
introduction to the sources.

THE 'SCALDS' AND THEIR POEMS

Among the sources considered most reliable, are scaldic poems
(lays) composed by the king's own court 'scalds' (bards).

Customarily the Norse kings and earls of the time kept scalds
in their pay — men whose special task was to compose poems
in praise of their lord's victories and other achievements. Possibly for reasons of tradition, practically all the scalds were
Icelanders. The poems were intended to spread the fame of a
ruler far and wide among his contemporaries, while securing
preservation for posterity.

A great many of these lays have, in point of fact, been
preserved and, in due time, recorded by the authors of sagas to
authenticate their stories. The long, formal poems composed for
special occasions are considered especially trustworthy.

It may be asked, how far can a poem of praise, made by an
underling in order to flatter and please his lord, be trusted?

The poems' general reliability is, however, confirmed by the
fact that they were recited at court; many of the men present
would know whether the praise given was excessive — if it
were, the poem would be considered derisive, the scald, in
consequence, losing his lord's favour.

THE TALE THE CHURCH TOLD

This story is only known in its fully developed form: as it was presented during the latter half of the twelfth century.

The most important text deals with the Saint's life and miracles: 'Passio et miracula beati Olavi', 'The suffering and miracles of Saint Olav' — abbreviated 'Passio Olavi'. The author, in all probability, was Øystein Erlendsson, archbishop of Nidaros (ancient name of Trondheim) during the period 1171—1189.

VARIOUS SAGAS

The oldest major saga describing the life of St Olav was written in Iceland, probably during the period 1160—80. Unfortunately, it has survived only in a few fragments.

There is, however, good reason to believe that a saga which has survived complete, the so-called Saga of Legends (the saga closes with a collection of legends about the Saint's miracles) is closely akin to the lost version. The Saga of Legends, also Icelandic, most probably dates back to the first decade of the thirteenth century.

Next there appears a veritable crowd of St Olav sagas, all put into writing during the 1220'ies. There is the saga written by the Icelander Styrmir, which has survived in fragments only, mostly as interpolated in various saga manuscripts. Again, there is the St Olav saga that forms part of the so-called 'Fagrskinna' ('the beautiful vellum', the name describing a manuscript unfortunately lost in the great fire of Copenhagen in 1728 — a copy did, however, survive); Fagrskinna was written by an unknown Icelander who seems to have visited Norway at that time. Further, there is the famous Snorri Sturluson's so-called 'Great Saga of St Olav', as well as a somewhat shorter version contained in his book on the lives of Norse kings.

King Olav's fleet. Woodcut by Hans Gerhard Sørensen, illustrating Fagrskinna, another book of sagas of Norwegian Kings (mentioned on page 57).

SUNDRY TEXTS

A number of chronicles and annals, English, German, French, Russian, contribute information of varying importance towards the understanding of our Saint.

The sources also include medieval laws — and a couple of runic inscriptions.

ON SCANDINAVIAN LETTERS

In Scandinavian names of people and places I shall use a few letters that may be unfamiliar to English-speaking readers. I hereby give those letters and their pronounciation:

å — pronounced as the a in ball.

ø — pronounced as the i in bird (ö is the Swedish letter for the same sound).

æ — approximately pronounced as the ai i hair (ä is the Swedish letter for the same sound).

In addition comes the Icelandic and old Norse letter ð, which I shall use in a couple of connections — ð is pronounced like th in weather.

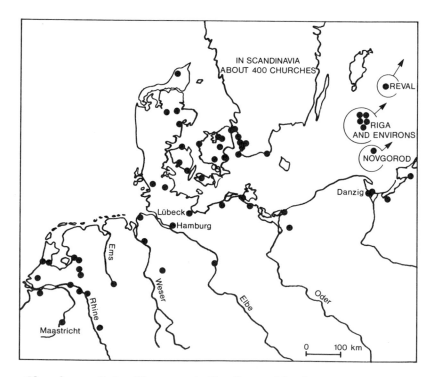

Churches to Saint Olav were built all over Northern Europe.

Olav, the Viking

First of all: what is a Viking?

Historians and specialists of the old Norse language have long debated the origin of the term, without coming to agreement. However, it is used in medieval Icelandic manuscripts much as it is employed today, i.e. as signifying a merciless marauder.

The word will be used here according to that definition.

Consulting the sources, let us begin with the scaldic poems.

SIGVAT THE SCALD

Most famous among king Olav's court scalds was — and is — an Icelander named Sigvat Tordarson, known as Sigvat 'the Scald', an honorific nickname.

Sigvat composed several major lays in praise of his king, the last one, a memorial poem, more than a decade after king Olav's death.

Sigvat's poems give the impression that he himself was truly a Christian. He did not take part in the king's last battle at Stiklestad, since he had gone on a pilgrimage to Rome. In a verse considered part of his memorial poem of king Olav, he relates:

Tired of battle I left
at home my gold-adorned sword
— that which the king gave me — ,
set out on the good journey.
Holy Rome was my goal;
I exchanged my costly sword,
the weapon that feeds wolves,
for a consecrated pilgrim's staff.

Those are strange words, indeed, from a Viking.

But, surprisingly enough, Sigvat does not mention the king's Christian faith until after his death. However, his own obvious faith bears abundant witness to it.

THE QUEEN'S ADMIRER

Another major poem about king Olav was composed by Ottar 'the black', Sigvat's nephew.

The poem has quite a story attached to it — a story rendered in the oldest sagas on the life of the king. According to what is generally accepted as a version of Styrmir's saga, it goes thus:

Ottar had been at the king of Sweden's court, and he had composed a love poem to Astrid, the Swedish king's daughter (who became Olav Haraldsson's wife). That poem king Olav intensely disliked; he was of the opinion that it praised the queen in an unseemly manner. Later, when Ottar came to Norway, the king had him thrown in gaol.

Sigvat the Scald was closely related to Ottar and a great friend of his. During the night he went to Ottar in prison and asked how he felt.

Ottar replied that he had known greater happiness.

Sigvat asked him to recite the poem he had made in praise of queen Astrid, and Ottar did so.

Sigvat said: 'You have certainly used strong words, and I am not surprised that the king dislikes your poem. But let us change the verses a bit. Then you should compose a lay lauding the king. For he will certainly ask you to recite your love poem, and when he has heard it, he will want to kill you. However, as soon as you come to the end, you must start reciting your poem in praise of *him* — don't let anything stop you!'

Ottar followed Sigvat's advice; during the three nights and days he spent in prison, he composed a poem in praise of king Olav.

The task accomplished, he was taken to the king and greeted him in a most seemly manner. But king Olav did not acknowledge his greeting; he said:

'Now, Ottar, you must recite the poem you have made about queen Astrid. She shall hear how highly you praise her.'

Astrid sat next to the king.

Ottar sat down at the king's feet and did as he had been told. The king, listening, blushed scarlet. But Ottar did not let that disturb him; when he came to the end of the last verse, he immediately went on with his poem in honour of the king.

The king's guardsmen cried out for Ottar to stop.

But Sigvat said: 'It should be obvious to all that the king will decide Ottar's fate. He must decide, also, whether or not Ottar shall be allowed to recite his poem. As for us, it will do us good to hear our king praised.'

The guardsmen were pacified, Ottar went on. Meanwhile the king sat silent.

When the poem was finished, Sigvat praised it highly.

The king said: 'I advise you, Ottar, to ask for your head in reward for that poem.'

Ottar replied: 'That seems to me a good reward, even though the head is not very beautiful.'

The king then pulled a gold ring off his own arm and gave it to Ottar.

But Astrid slid a gold ring off her finger and gave it to Ottar.

The king said to the queen: 'Do you reward mockery with a gift of friendship?'

Astrid retorted: 'You should not be angry with me because of this. I reward my praise, you rewarded yours.'

The king said: 'Let us leave it at that.'

Sagas are not necessarily trustworthy. However, the story of Ottar and his poem is interesting in more ways than one.

It points to the value of a good poem in those days — even to a king. Furthermore, the exchange between the king and queen Astrid is a contest of words concerning what is to be considered praise, and what, being excessive as such, is to be considered mockery. The king's courage and great deeds had been praised, while, in the case of queen Astrid, one may surmise (Ottar's poem to her unfortunately is lost) that the poem alluded to her charms and beauty. Most probably the love poem was forgot because the scald had used terms that were considered indecent by the standards of a later age.

Seen in such a context, the queen's retort is truly devastating.

But we shall return to the more reliable sources: Sigvat's and Ottar's poems.

BATTLES, BATTLES, BATTLES!

Scaldic poetry is composed according to certain rules. With reference to the major poems made by the scalds in honour of their lords, that means, among other things, that they relate the main events of a man's life, and only by implication give glimpses of his personality. Indeed, to people of those times, the main events of a chieftain's life were the battles in which he had taken part. In one of his lays Sigvat follows Olav Haraldsson from one major battle to another, even numbering them — beginning with the first time the king 'reddened the wolf's paw in blood' (the first time he killed in battle) and ending, in the poem as we know it today, with the king's thirteenth battle. The battle of Stiklestad is mentioned as his twentieth in another of Sigvat's lays.

I shall, however, not quote Sigvat's poems here. Instead I shall attempt to translate some of the verses that Ottar com-

From the Snorri illustrations: young Olav Haraldsson leaving Norway to plunder and kill in foreign lands. With him is Rane, his trusted adviser and foster father.

posed. He is the more dramatic of the two bards — Sigvat is of a less flamboyant temperament.

Scaldic poetry is composed according to very strict rules of rhyme and meter. For this purpose I will, however, generally neglect the rules of composition and concentrate on the contents — and clarity.

About king Olav's youth, Ottar has this to say:

> Young did you turn the ocean's
> dun horse towards Denmark,
> king, courageous in battle!
> Your token: tremendous deeds.

'The ocean's dun horse' is the ship.

> With shimmering oars you rowed
> your ship on the Baltic sea
> . . .
> People were sorely afeard
> wherever you went, lord;
> the ravens were well fed
> where you ravaged the coasts.

The two scalds, who convey much the same information, then give an account of marauding in Sweden, Finland, Denmark and the Netherlands.

Whereafter Olav's ships take him to England:

> Great one, you broke London's
> bridge in the storm of Odin;
> the golden lands of the dragon
> you conquered, mighty king.

The term 'storm of Odin' (in the original 'Yggs veðr', 'the storm of the terrible one' — 'Yggr' was one of Odin's, i.e. Oden's, names) is a paraphrase for 'battle', and is interesting because it shows that king Olav did not (as had an earlier Christian king of Norway) forbid the mentioning of pagan gods in poems dedicated to him. 'The golden lands of the dragon' is another paraphrase, meaning 'rich lands' — dragons supposedly brooded on hoards of gold.

According to Snorri Sturluson, the great Icelandic writer of sagas, the story of London bridge ran as follows:

Roofing his ships with the material of houses he had torn down, Olav shielded his men from the stones and other missiles thrown and shot down by the people standing on the bridge. Thus protected, the ships were rowed in under the bridge, and ropes were fastened around the poles on which it was built.

From the Snorri illustrations: an artist's conception of how London bridge was torn down by king Olav and his men.

Then Olav and his men rowed downstream, using all their strength. The poles were pulled from under the bridge, which fell, plunging its defenders into the water.

The Anglo-Saxon Chronicles point out that in the year 1009 'there came that immense enemy force, which we call Thurkil's force'. 'Thurkil' is Torkjell Høye ('the tall'), a Danish chieftain. According to the poems of Sigvat and Ottar, Olav must have been another chieftain of that 'immense enemy force', and the Saga of Legends mentions Torkjell by name as his companion in England. The Chronicles further state that London was attacked several times that year, but not conquered. And it is interesting to note that Ottar praises Olav's feat of tearing the bridge down, but he does not claim victory for the king over the town's defenders.

Concerning another battle, fought in East Anglia, Ottar has this comment:

> Lord, on the battlefield your army
> flung the enemy corpses into heaps.

And of Canterbury, town of the archbishop, Ottar reports:

Yngve, you won the great
battle against descendants of kings.
Good king, one morning
you conquered Canterbury.
Fire and smoke played
mightily over the town;
son of a king, your victory
shortened the lives of many.

The use of the name 'Yngve' for the king is interesting here —
we shall return to that in another connection, since it designates
the pagan god of fertility from whom Olav was supposedly
descended. It is remarkable that the king, who was presumably
a Christian when that poem was made, did not protest at the
allusion.

Other places named as sites for king Olav's battles are found
in France and Spain.

THE MAKING OF ANOTHER SAINT

Now, let us return to the sack of Canterbury and consider that
event from the point of view of Anglo-Saxon and English
chronicle writers.

Of the 'immense enemy force' which, we must presume,
included king Olav, the Anglo-Saxon Chronicles tell that it was
still ravaging England in the year 1011, and 'men made truce
and treaty with them. Nevertheless, for all this truce, treaty
and tribute they went everywhere in raiding bands, and plundered and killed our wretched folk'.

Canterbury was attacked in September of that year:

In this year, between the Nativity of St Mary and Michaels-
mas, they besieged Canterbury, and got in by deceit . . .

Anglo-Saxon Chronicles relate: 'In this year (793) fierce, foreboding omens came over the land of Northumbria, and wretchedly terrified people. There were excessive whirlwinds, lighting storms, and fiery dragons were seen flyig in the sky. These signs were shortly followed by great famine, and shortly after in the same year, on January 8th, the ravaging of heathen men destroyed God's church at Lindisfarne through brutal robbery and slaughter.'

That attack on a defenceless monastery is generally regarded as the beginning of the 'Viking Age.' And on this stone from Lindisfarne the Vikings are depicted as they appeared to those monks – and undoubtedly to people of England and other lands attacked some two hundred years later by Olav Haraldsson and his men.

There they seized archbishop Aelfeah . . . Inside, they seized all the people in holy orders, men and women — it is impossible to say how many people that was — and stayed in that town as long as they wished. When they had explored the borough completely, they went to the ships and took the archbishop with them. Then he was captive who had been England's head, and Christendom's, until the time they martyred him.

This sounds fairly peaceful, compared to Ottar's account of a fire and the death of many. Another chronicler, Florence of Worcester (year of birth unknown, died in A.D. 1118), does, however, give additional information, and is also more in accord with Ottar:

On the twentieth day of the siege, part of the town was set on fire by a traitor ... the army forced its way in and conquered it. Some people were killed by sword, others died in the fire, many, also, were thrown from the top of the town wall ... Married women were pulled by their hair through the streets of the town to be burnt alive. Infants were torn from their mother's breast, killed by spears or crushed under the wheels of heavy carts.
At the same time the intruders made archbishop Aelfeah a prisoner, chaining him and tormenting him in many ways.

Florence goes on to tell that nine out of ten of the townspeople were killed — whereupon the town was plundered, and what was left of it was burned.

The archbishop was kept prisoner until shortly after Easter the following year (1012). On his death the Anglo-Saxon Chronicles, quoted here, are in agreement with Florence:

On the Saturday, the force became greatly stirred up against the bishop, because he would promise them no tribute, and forbade that anyone give them ransom for him; they were also very drunk because of the southern wine that had been brought. They seized the bishop, took him to their meeting place on Sunday, the evening of Easter (i.e. a week after Easter Sunday), and pelted him to death with bones and cattle's heads. One of them struck him with the back of an axe on the head, so that with the blow he sank down and his holy blood fell on the earth, and his holy soul was sent to God's kingdom.

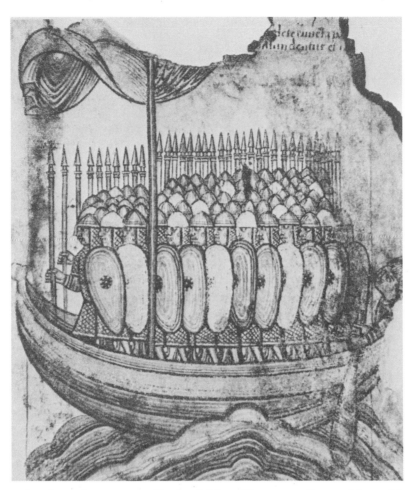

After his adventures in England king Olav, according to his scalds and to the French chronicler Guillaume of Jumièges, turned to France. Scaldic lays tell of his raiding along the coast of Aquitaine, among other places. This illustration (from an 11th century manuscript from Anjou) shows how the Vikings may have appeared to the French.

In France, however, fate caught up with king Olav – he was baptised in Rouen, probably in the year 1013.

The dead Aelfeah was, not surprisingly, revered as a martyr and Saint by his countrymen.

THE ART OF EXTORTION

An important aspect of Viking strategy was to demand payment for *not* attacking, or for what was euphemistically called 'protection'. The English, in the last decade of the tenth and the first decade of the eleventh century, were thus induced to pay immense sums to Danish and Norwegian Vikings.

Ottar bears witness to the fact that Olav Haraldsson was no stranger to these tactics:

> Men of English descent
> lacked the strength needed
> to resist you, great lord,
> and *you* did not spare them for taxes.
> Often people had to
> give gold to the good king,
> they gathered in great flocks
> on the beaches to render their tribute.

ON CRUELTY AND GREED

Viking cruelty is notorious; so is Viking greed. Pagan Scandinavians lacked the restraint that Christianity is credited with imposing on people's inclination to rob and kill, to maim and torture. Their gods demanded neither humility nor charity from them; being cruel and deceitful to enemies simply formed part of their ideal, one might almost say, their creed. And they were impelled by a totally unrestrained appetite for wealth and power.

For Olav Haraldsson, the acquisition of wealth was a necessary premise to his plan of conquering the land of his ancestor king Harald Hårfagre. A king needed soldiers if he were to take a country and submit it to his rule, and silver was required in order to pay those soldiers. With one exception the kings of Norway, preceeding and including Olav Haraldsson, had made themselves fortunes from plunder and extortion. (And, just for the record, the single exception had been sorely hampered by his dependence on the aristocracy.)

Olav Haraldsson certainly knew what he was about when he started his quest for the crown by building up a fortune.

A VIKING KING

It would be amazing if a man with Olav's background were to become mild and meek, all of a sudden, through a change in faith.

According to the sagas, no such transformation took place; the king brought his old cruel ways as well as his new faith, back to Norway with him.

Furthermore, since resistance to conversion was considered by him as equal to rebellion, brutality became an expression of his missionary zeal. — Of this the sagas give so many examples that little doubt can remain.

Altar-front (originally from the Haltdalen Church in the district of Trøndelag, now in the Trondheim cathedral). Probably done in Trondheim, the painting dates from the first half of the 14th century. The Saint carries his usual attribute, an ax. Lower left: Shortly before the battele at Stiklestad the Saint pays to have masses said for his enemies. Upper left: The night before the battle he dreams of ascending a ladder towards heaven. Lower right: He dies on the battlefield. Upper right: He is enshrined.

The Saint of the Church

We shall now encounter an entirely different Olav Haraldsson — as different from the Viking as day is from night.

OLAV HARALDSSON CANONIZED

The Saga of Legends is our source:

> When king Olav had been killed (in the battle of Stiklestad), they carried his body from the battleground in the evening, and they washed it. A blind man came to the place and washed his eyes in the water that was now mixed with the king's blood. And straight away he was able to see. . . .
>
> Later the king was buried close to Kristkirken (the Christ church of Nidaros, now Trondheim — but here the saga is mistaken, Kristkirken had not yet been built). His body stayed in the grave for one year and five days. By that time it had risen out of the ground. Wise men counseled that the king's body should be buried a second time. They all prayed to God that he would reveal Olav's holiness by letting the body rise again. Nine nights later his body had risen a second time and he had thus been proven holy. . . .
>
> This time bishop Grimkjell removed the body of king Olav from the grave. . . . A crowd had gathered. And at the advice of bishop Grimkjell and king Svein (king Knut's son, vassal king of Norway during the period 1030—35) a strand of hair was taken from his beard, and some blood came with it. The hair was placed in consecrated fire, and it did not burn. . . .
>
> After that king Olav was placed in a shrine and shown much reverence, and marvellous miracles took place.

King Svein was a young boy under the guardianship of his mother, queen Alfiva (Aelfgifu), who was king Knut's concubine and had come to Norway from England with her son. A later saga (Snorri Sturluson's saga of St Olav) presents queen Alfiva as a kind of 'devil's advocate'; she questions the procedure at every step, but is put to shame for her scepticism.

POEMS OF A NEW KIND

Exactly what happened during the first couple of years following Olav Haraldsson's death, cannot be established after an interval of nearly a thousand years. It is, however, certain that a remarkable change in popular opinion took place — contemporary testimony is provided by scaldic lays composed during the 1030'ies and 1040'ies.

As early as in 1032 or 1033 the scald Torarin Lovtunge ('of the praising tongue'), an Icelander who lived in Nidaros/ Trondheim at the time, describes the king's reliquiary thus:

> There rests
> the highly praised king,
> immaculate, guiltless,
> his body unhurt.
> His hair is growing,
> his nails as well,
> like the hair and nails
> of a living man.

There above
the altar, high,
candles burn
to honour Christ.
Thus Olav,
free from sin,
saved his soul
before he died.

At that shrine
flocks of cripples
seek the aid
of the Saint;
the blind, the dumb
and the maimed pray
for his intercession
— healed they leave.

Here, just a couple of years after the battle of Stiklestad, Olav Haraldsson, once chased from his country and then killed by his countrymen when he attempted a 'comeback', is proclaimed a miracle-making Saint. However, little is said of the king's life — only that he 'free from sin / saved his soul / before he died'. And Torarin does not make clear when or how the king is supposed to have saved his soul.

Sigvat the Scald, who composed his great memorial poem to king Olav in the 1040'ies, concludes by telling the same story of holiness and miracles. He also mentions one event that may partly account for people's change of heart:

> A marvellous miracle happened
> the day of the king's death:
> though the sky was clear, the sun
> deprived the men of its rays.
> The day was robbed of its colour
>
> . . .
>
> From the East I heard of the battle.

The poem's 'battle' is the battle of Stiklestad, about which Sigvat, who was absent, heard 'from the East'. And the 'marvellous miracle' refers to a solar eclipse that took place in the summer of the year 1030 and was observed as a total one in the area of the battlefield.

There is, however, one major objection to the poem's identification of battle with eclipse: the battle took place on July 29th, the eclipse on August 31st.

On that background some historians have suggested that the battle did not take place on the traditional date, but one month later. A more likely explanation, and the most widely accepted one, is that people of the time linked the eclipse to the battle — in spite of the few weeks separating the two events. In general they were inclined to superstition and knew very little about eclipses — to them it must have seemed obvious that king Olav's God was angry with them for slaying the king.

Sigvat himself was, no doubt, in good faith. By the time he returned to Norway, the two events were probably presented as inseparably linked.

ST OLAV ON THE INTERNATIONAL SCENE

According to foreign sources the Saint's fame spread far and wide — and in an amazingly short period of time.

The oldest English liturgical text for the feast of St Olav dates back to the 1050'ies (then as now his feast day was July 29th). And the German historian Adam of Bremen, who wrote in the 1070'ies, mentions St Olav. He relates how pilgrims from far away sought to the Saint's shrine, where 'great miracles of healing' took place.

THE OFFICIAL VERSION

A hundred years or so later, the Church's version of Saint Olav's life had taken shape and found its expression in the Passio Olavi. The text, recording the Saint's 'suffering and miracles', exists in two versions, both originally written in latin. However, the older and shorter one was soon translated into the vernicular.

Passio Olavi begins with a short life story of the Saint. I shall render, in part, this story according to the longer version of the Passio — it provides amazing reading when one recalls Ottar's and Sigvat's poems as well as the sagas, and also the fact that king Olav had a son born out of wedlock.

However, examining the text, one notes that it contains quite a few passages from the Bible — the author presents a biblical interpretation of the king's life. In fact, he presents a biblical interpretation also of the North, as a symbol, starting out with a whole series of Bible texts concerning the North as a source of evil. Archbishop Øystein, the probable author, does not always identify those texts as quotations from the Bible. That

36

Towards the end of the twelfth century this picture of Saint Olav was painted on one of the columns of the Church of the Nativity in Bethlehem.

information, which is rather important to anyone who wants to grasp the author's intention, will, however, be given here (I shall quote the Bible according to the King James version):

At the time when the famous king Olav was ruler of Norway, a very large country towards the north with Denmark to the south, there came to that land 'the feet of him that bringeth good tidings, that publisheth peace, that bringeth good tidings of good.' (Isaiah 52:7). Until then the peoples there had sacrificed to pagan gods and had been led astray by errors and superstition. They had certainly heard of others who worshipped the one true God, but most of them had scornfully refused to believe. As they live close to the north wind, they are near also to the author of evil, who made their hearts freeze in an unbelief hard as ice. For, as Jeremiah perceived in a vision, he who worries and complains so much: 'I see a seething pot, and the face thereof is toward the north,' and 'Out of the north an evil shall break forth upon all the inhabitants of the land.' (Jeremiah 1:13—14). Furthermore: 'I (i.e. Lucifer) will exalt my throne above the stars of God: I will sit also upon the mount of the congregation, in the sides of the north.' (Isaiah 14:13)

But the great and highly praised Lord, who builds his city in the remote north (alludes to Psalms 48:2—3), assuaged the severe northern storm by mild winds from the south; finally he mollified those self-assertive and savage people with the warmth of the faith. . . .

Of this country king Olav was the ruler, as has been said. He was a pagan, but nevertheless of a noble mind, and so good that he always was willing to do that which was right. He was converted in England and experienced the truth of God's words. He took the faith to heart, and with a mind inspired by God he hurried towards the grace of baptism, which he received at Rouen. As soon as he was cleansed in that saving bath, he became a different man, 'buried with Christ by baptism into death,' as the apostle says (Romans 6:4); 'forgetting those things which are behind, and reaching forth unto those things which are before'. (Philippians 3:13),

Up to the time of the Reformation St Olav's shrine in Nidaros (now Trondheim) was much sought by pilgrims. The Saint with his ax and a pilgrim are portrayed on a reliquiary (Hedal Church, Valdres around the year 1250).

he began a new life in close observance of the faith he now professed. He turned away from all empty pleasures, and to his eyes the earthly kingdom's glory paled compared to the sweet happiness of the heavenly. Even though he lived the luxurious life of a king, he was poor in spirit; even though he was burdened with earthly cares, his mind was set on heavenly things. He turned away from all that which God's law forbids, and that which God's law bids us to do, was his greatest pleasure.

Not content with being saved himself, he laboured with care and zeal to convert the people that God's providence had submitted to his rule. The strange thing happened that he, who was king, took it upon himself also to carry out the work of an apostle — in the capacity of chief speaker (refers to Acts 14:12 and St Paul's preaching), he preached the grace of Christ to many people in many places. With his marvellous gift of speech, a grace of God, he persuaded some to give up their shameless sacrifices to pagan gods, and he taught them to know and fear their Creator. His matchless zeal for God and the purity of his life so fired many that they felt contempt for the world and turned all their love towards their heavenly home. For who could be so stubborn and

Pilgrim badge of lead showing St Olav. Such badges were carried by pilgrims to indicate the shrine they sought or had visited, and were supposed to protect the wearer from molestation.

callous that he would not listen to the noble king and his mild words, so full of spiritual wisdom? Who could be so unwilling and indifferent that the king, with his gift of speech, did not awake him from his torpor?

But the king was surrounded by an unwise and evil people, and even though he managed to convert many, even more were his enemies — mighty men who were impelled more by selfishness than by the fear of God, more by habit than by wisdom, more by evil desires than by the love of truth. With all their might they resisted the proclamation of God's word and the good works of Christ's noble martyr, and tried to make rough the even paths of the Lord (alludes to Isaiah 40:3). But *he* was just, as confident as a lion he knew no fear (alludes to Proverbs 38:1). Like the blessed Job before him, he 'did not fear a great multitude' (Job 31:34); nor did he fear the ridicule of his intimates.

This is a fair sample. Passio Olavi goes on, in an equally florid and biblical style, to describe the king's yearning for the crown of martyrdom, his exile and death at the hands of 'the enemies of truth' who took 'counsel together against the Lord, and against his anointed' (Psalms 2:2). It is further pointed out that 'he, who loved peace, was forced to fight for the sake of justice'.

It should be fairly obvious that our Saint has been pressed into a biblical role that may have fitted him better in retrospect than it did in real life.

It is, however, interesting to note that, in the Passio Olavi, there is no confusion of the solar eclipse and the battle of Stiklestad. Was the learned author possibly aware that the two did not coincide?

The rest of the Passio Olavi is a recital of the Saint's many miracles. One will suffice:

There were two brothers, men of noble birth, who possessed plenty of riches. They had a sister; she was beautiful, but not very careful of her reputation, as time was to show.

St Olav healing the maimed English priest. Detail from a diptych (early 14th century, place of origin: Norway)

She became friendly with an English priest who lived at her brothers' house, and in all seemliness she was of service to him. However, it so happened that evil gossip arose concerning the girl. And since people always listen eagerly to that kind of loose talk, the innocent priest was thought to be guilty — if only for the reason that he and the girl often conversed together.

Because of the friendship between the priest and their sister, her brothers were almost convinced of the priest's guilt. They became very angry, but hid their feelings.

One day the two brothers sent for the priest, who anticipated no evil. They brought with them one of their sworn men, who had been informed of the wrong they were meditating, and they took the priest along as if they wanted his assistance in some negotiations.

When they had advanced into a remote place, they attacked the priest, who was quite unprepared; they broke his legs, cut his tongue out and tore his eyes out of his head. When, in fear and pain, he began to make noises, using the stub of his tongue, they assailed him again, wrenching the stub of his tongue out with tongs, and cut it shorter. Then they left him there, half dead.

The St Olav of the late Middle Ages (Hammerfest Church place of origin: Germany). The human figure under his feet (ill. page 8) has now been replaced by a dragon the head of which resembles the king's head — the meaning of this symbol is obscure. It is also characteristic of the period (around year 1500) that the Saint is dressed in armour.

A poor woman took him to her house.

Even though the priest had suffered such a terrible fate at the hands of men, he did not lose his faith in God's mercy. His mouth was silent, but he spoke the more fervently with a heart wholly given to God, and the weaker he was, the stronger and more mighty he became. He directed all his prayers to the glorious martyr Olav, of whom he had heard that he worked great miracles; he implored him not to abandon him in his misery.

The more miserable he was, the more was he deserving of compassion; the more he was filled with dread, the more fervent became his prayers. Thus he prayed to the martyr continually, begging for his help — sighing, humble and miserable.

The next day he finally fell into restfull sleep. And behold! the holy man to whom he had humbly prayed, came to him in a vision, saying that he was the Olav to whom he had directed his humble and fervent prayers. The Saint stroked gently his legs, his eyes and all other places where he suffered pain. Last he grabbed the stub of his tongue and pulled it so hard that the priest cried out in pain. But as soon as the martyr had touched the poor, maimed man with his healing hand, a feeling of God's care streamed through him so abundantly that he felt no suffering of any kind. He recovered his tongue, his legs were healed, his eyes came back into his head, and all the other sores with which he was stricken, were made well.

But as a proof that his eyes had been torn out, he always had a white scar on each eyelid.

The King of Pagan Myth

The older St Olav sagas, the Saga of Legends and that of Styrmir, are generally inspired by the Church's tale of the pious Saint. There are, however, exceptions from that rule: the older sagas contain a fair amount of material concerning pagan myths.

Myth, legend, and historical facts mingle in the narrative of these sagas, and the borderline between them is often obscure.

Concerning the probable date of these myths: some, on the evidence of a famous scaldic poem, Ynglingatal, quoted by Snorri Sturluson in his saga of Norse kings, go back to the year 900. Others we know only from the above mentioned sagas, and their age extending beyond that of the sagas may be surmised, although not proved, on the basis of their pagan inspiration.

However, prior to our entering the somewhat hazy land of these myths, I shall provide a few pieces of background information.

DESCENDANT OF GODS

Snorri Sturluson quotes the lay Ynglingatal in 'Ynglingesaga', which opens his collected sagas of the Norse kings. The poem is attributed to the Norwegian scald Tjodolv from Kvine (a place in the district of Vest-Agder), and its name signifies 'The enumeration of the Ynglings'.

According to medieval sources the poem was composed some time around the year 900 in honour of a Harald Olavsson, a cousin of Harald Hårfagre's.

Burial mounds near Uppsala, Sweden – resting place of some of St Olav's supposed forebears, the Uppsala kings. According to the lay Ynglingatal, most of those men suffered strange fates – one, for instance, drowned in a vat of mead, another was hanged by his wife in a necklace.

The lay, as Snorri quotes it, enumerates 27 generations beginning with Fjolne, the son of Yngve-Frøy, and ending with a king Olav nicknamed Digre ('the fat', 'the loudmouth' — or 'the physically big') or Digerbein ('with the big leg' or, more probably, 'with the large frame', 'the physically big'), the father of Harald Olavsson and an half-uncle of Harald Hårfagre's.

However, Frøy (i.e. Frey) was the Norse god of fertility, and Yngve, meaning 'chieftain', supposedly was one of his names — hence the name 'Ynglings' for the men descended from him, and 'Yngve' used as an honorary title by his descendants. This, then, is the 'Yngve' applied by the scald Ottar to king Olav Haraldsson, who belonged to the Yngling clan.

Within many pagan traditions the claim to royal birth is founded on a claim of descendancy from the gods; this also applies in pagan Scandinavia, where, according to sagas and scaldic poems, the royal families were thought to descend from the gods Frøy and/or Odin.

And while Olav Haraldsson claimed a certain territory, i.e. a large part of present-day Norway, as his inheritance from Harald Hårfagre, his — and Harald Hårfagre's — claim to kinghood must, in the eyes of his contemporaries, have been founded on his descendancy from the god Frøy.

THE KING WHO BECAME A DEITY

The above mentioned Olav Digre, Harald Hårfagre's uncle, was the ruler of a kingdom on both sides of the Oslo fjord. In time he died, an event hardly surprising in itself. However, according to the older sagas, and more surprisingly, he predicted his own death. (The story, incidentally, is not substantiated by Ynglingatal's scald, Tjodolv from Kvine.) Olav Digre was buried in a mound near his home — with Tjodolv as their source the sagas name the place Geirstad — at some time during the latter half of the ninth century.

Evidently he had been a very popular king, for after his death people gave him a new name, Olav Geirstad-alv, and transformed him into some kind of deity to whom they offered sacrifices. Within Norse paganism, the 'alv's were second only to the gods in the hierarchy of supernatural beings, and they possibly (although here we are reduced to conjecture) had the power to increase the fertility of the soil. Frøy, the god of fertility, is said to live at Alvheim, 'the home of the alvs'.

A FAITHLESS HUSBAND AND FATHER

According to all the sagas, Olav Haraldsson's father was Harald Grenske (i.e. from the district of Grenland some 100 miles southwest of Oslo), and Harald was the great-grandson of Harald Hårfagre. He married a woman named Åsta, of whom the sources know very little, except that her father's name was Gudbrand Kula.

Carved dragon's head from the region of Vestfold, (first half of the 9th century). Vestfold was the homeland of Olav the Geirstad-alv. This sculpture was found in the mound where the famous Oseberg ship was buried.

Harald, however, regretted the match, thinking that he could have done better. Consequently, he sent Åsta back to her father, an act which amounted to a terrible insult to her and all her clan. Thereafter he went to Sweden in the hope of finding himself a more suitable wife.

However, things did not work out that way. The hopeful suitor met his death in Sweden, leaving Åsta in a state of fury — and also pregnant.

A THOUSAND YEAR OLD GHOST STORY

We shall now see how these sundry pieces of information reappear as part of the pagan myth concerning king Olav Haraldsson. I translate from the Saga of Legends, albeit somewhat abridged — adding, in parenthesis, some words of explanation:

A man by the name of Rane had been highly trusted in the service of the king (Harald Grenske). One night Rane dreamed that a chieftain wearing a cloak made of precious foreign cloth, came to him.

'Wake up, Rane!' the chieftain said.

Rane replied that he was awake.

'No,' the other one said. 'You are not. You only think you are. I am king Olav Digre, and I have come to ask you a favour.

Break open my burial mound at Geirstad, and bring along with you steel and tinder (to light a torch), a rope and a heavy stick! (Open the mound from the top, and lay the stick across the opening.) Then tie the rope to the stick and let yourself down into the mound by it.

Inside the mound you will see a man dressed exactly as I am. Walk up to him and take from him the ring around his arm, his sword and his belt with his knife attached! You will see many men to his right and to his left. But have courage, do as I have told you, and you shall suffer no harm. Next you must cut his head off. If you do not, you will come to a terrible end. Once that is done, you will be wise to leave the mound as fast as possible.

Afterwards, go to the home of Gudbrand Kula. There you will find Åsta, his daughter, in childbirth and unable to bring forth her child. If they ask you for advice, then tell them to place my belt around her. And say that in return for your help you want to name the child.'

Rane does as he has been told by the Olav Digre of his dream. He goes to the burial mound at Geirstad to fetch the Geirstad-alv's arm-ring, sword, belt and knife. He continues to Gudbrand

Burial mounds at Borre — where most of the Vestfold forebears of St Olav are supposed to have been buried.

Kula's farm, and is well received. Åsta Gudbrandsdotter (i.e. the daughter of Gudbrand) is in the throes of a difficult childbirth. Rane lays the dead man's belt around her — whereupon she immediately gives birth to a son.

The father of the child is Harald Grenske, and Gudbrand, not wishing to foster the son of that faithless rascal, is of a mind to kill the boy. This Rane manages to prevent — he becomes the boy's foster father and names him Olav after Olav Digre. As a 'name-gift' (it was customary to give a child a gift on such an occasion) Rane endows him with the Geirstad-alv's belt and knife and his arm-ring. Later on this new Olav also is given the dead man's sword, which is known in the sagas by two names (weapons were actually given names): 'Bæsing', i.e. 'son of outlawed mother', and 'Neite', i.e. 'the piercing one' or 'the conqueror'.

A VERY SPECIAL SWORD

At any rate one conclusion may be drawn from the myth:

Olav Haraldsson most probably possessed a sword that was feared as well as admired — a sword that his contemporaries linked with his namesake Olav Digre the Geirstad-alv.

He may, in fact, have owned the same Olav's sword, taken from his burial mound — archaeological evidence shows that such mounds have been broken into during pagan times. And the tradition of Olav Geirstad-alv's sword must have been strong indeed, since it became part of the fundamentally Christian early St Olav sagas.

What, one may ask, would such a sword have meant to a Christian king? According to Snorri's saga and other sources, Olav Haraldsson kept the sword all his life, finally carrying it into battle at Stiklestad.

In addition to being an excellent weapon, it most likely acted as a symbol of his descendancy from pagan gods. It is also highly probable that it was considered a magical sword, which endowed the man who wielded it with the promise of victory.

Viking swords — and other weapons of the period.

ON REINCARNATION

Pagan Norsemen believed in reincarnation — not as a general rule, but for a few, chosen persons. Seen in that perspective, the myth relates that people believed Olav Digre, the Geirstad-alv, to be reborn in Olav Haraldsson.

Indeed, naming the boy after the former Olav indicates that much — considered on a background of the general customs and beliefs of the period. A story derived from Styrmir's saga corroborates that interpretation:

> People say that one day king Olav (Haraldsson) and his bodyguard rode past Olav Geirstad-alv's burial mound. One of the guardsmen said:
>
> 'Tell me, lord, if you were once buried here.'
>
> The king replied: 'My soul never had two bodies; neither does it now, nor shall it on the day of Resurrection. If I told you otherwise, I should not be of the Church's faith.'
>
> The guardsman went on: 'People have mentioned that when you came to this place before, you said: Here we were, and from this place we set out.'
>
> The king retorted: 'Those words I have never uttered and will never utter.'
>
> However, the king was very upset; he spurred his horse and left the place in great haste.

The nickname 'Digre' in itself bears witness to the belief that Olav Haraldsson was the older Olav reborn — in the sagas and some of the scaldic poems, the younger Olav is also known as Olav Digre.

Digre may, as mentioned above, mean the physically big, but according to the sources St Olav was a man of no more than average height — the appellation thus interpreted would therefore be misleading. And in its other interpretations Digre is certainly not flattering, meaning 'the fat' or 'the loudmouth'; one might surmise it to be a nickname given Olav Haraldsson by his enemies.

But that is obviously not the case. Sigvat the Scald, who was among the king's closest friends, calls him by that name in his great memorial poem. And it is inconceivable that Sigvat, in that composition, should wish to deride his beloved king.

Consequently, Digre must have been an appellative pleasing to the king. In which case the conclusion is very close at hand: Olav the Saint himself believed he was the first Olav Digre, a pagan deity, reborn, and for that reason considered the appellative a name of honour.

Which would be sensational indeed and certainly raises the question: how Christian was our Saint?

Saint and King — a rational Picture

The views presented of Olav Haraldsson thus far have been essentially different from one another. Olav, the Viking, and the Olav of pagan myth may, true enough, represent facets of the same personality. But the Saint of the Church is of an altogether different species.

Now, let us see how the saga writers handled that problem.

St Olav sculptured in stone above the western entrance to the Eidsberg Church (latter half of the 13th century).

MYTH, LEGEND — AND HISTORY

In the older sagas myth and legend are intermingled with history. However, the Saga of Legends occasionally volunteers bits of information that break radically with the Church's representation of the Saint; the reader glimpses something beyond, which may be the remnant of a much earlier tradition.

On one occasion the saga generally describes the king in entire conformity with Church tradition; he is, for instance, said to be 'mild and humble, good-natured and considerate, generous and charitable, kind and careful not to commit sins'. But with that on record, the saga very surprisingly also states that many people considered the king 'a man wilful and powerseeking, harsh and hostile, stubborn and miserly, nasty and obstinate, haughty and proud to a fault' — which is a different story indeed.

As if to underscore this other version, the Saga of Legends puts the following words into the king's mouth — at the time he is being driven from his country by his own people: 'I admit that in many ways I have governed this country harshly and with violence.'

The Saga of Legends makes no attempt at reconciling those two quite different portraits of the king. They are left for the reader to ponder — which readers certainly have done.

The nineteenth century's leading authority on Norwegian history, P. A. Munch, translated the flattering part of the saga's statement in his 'History of the Norwegian People'. But the less flattering opinion of the Saint he did not translate. He presented that in old Norse in a footnote — explaining that the alliteration of pairs of words made translation too difficult. However, the words in praise of the king, which he *did* translate, have the same kind of alliteration.

A NEW POINT OF VIEW

During the 1220'ies a couple of sagawriters emerged who were not over-impressed by the Church's exaggerated account of the humble and pious St Olav, nor inclined to believe myths that they regarded as a product of pagan superstition.

Rationalism, 'medieval style', had arrived on the saga scene.

THE 'CUT TO THE BONE' SAGA

Of Fagrskinna, which is contemporary with Snorri's sagas, it may be said that it is written by an extremely sober, if unfortunately anonymous, author. In this book, containing sagas of Norse kings, he relates what he considers historical facts and generally leaves out whatever he judges to be unimportant — myths, legends. As a result he presents a short, rather dry version of the St Olav story — often the dry bones only, and at times hardly even those.

The author of Fagrskinna may, in the critical approach to his sources, be considered as a forerunner of modern historians.

One reason why he did not follow the tradition of the ecclesiastically inspired St Olav sagas, may have been that, while those earlier sagas seem to have been written by men in the service of the Church, *his* allegiance most probably was to Håkon Håkonsson, king of Norway during the period 1217—1263.

The original title of his compilation of sagas was 'Nóregs konunga tal', 'The enumeration of Norway's kings'.

SNORRI — HISTORIAN, AUTHOR, POLITICIAN

Snorri Sturluson was no less a rationalist; he did, however, write an entirely different saga about Olav Haraldsson.

Snorri was a very learned man according to the standards of his time. And, in addition to being the most famous of medieval Icelandic historians, he was a politician and a scald.

Snorri was born in the year 1178 or 1179, and belonged to a highly respected family. He married a wealthy woman, but, parting company with her, lived on a basis of common ownership with another rich woman. During a period he was Iceland's wealthiest man.

His known writings include, in addition to the Great Saga of St Olav and the Sagas of Norse Kings, a book of instruction in the composition of scaldic poetry. The latter contains a copious introduction to the pagan religion of Scandinavia.

St Olav on a processional banner from the period 1440–70 – depicted with his ax, his dragon and a hanap (an elaborate goblet or cup, here with a cover – an attribute of St Olav during the late Middle Ages, its connection with the Saint is obscure). The banner could, incidentally, serve two purposes, on the reverse side is a picture of another Saint.

He travelled to Norway twice, first during the years 1218—20, and then again during the period 1237—39; on each occasion he also visited Sweden. He managed to get himself mixed up in Norwegian politics by befriending a man who was to become the Norwegian king Håkon Håkonsson's enemy, and by promising king Håkon to serve his cause in gaining control of Iceland.

However, Snorri appears not to have lived up to his promise. And when he left Norway in the year 1239, he did so against king Håkon's will. Two years later Snorri was killed by an assassin dispatched by the king — who, incidentally, in the early 1260'ies accomplished his aim of becoming the sovereign of Iceland.

SNORRI'S ST OLAV

It must have been as obvious to Snorri as it is to us today that the various portrayals of the Saint, those presented by scaldic poetry, by the Church and by pagan myth, do not easily add up to a coherent picture of a single person. Snorri set out to remedy that situation.

His sources were those mentioned above, most likely with the exception of Fagrskinna. The saga writer Styrmir even was his house guest during one period, possibly while Styrmir composed his St Olav saga. In addition Snorri may have picked up a few bits of information, not likely to be of great importance, during his travels in Norway and Sweden.

He must have gone through these sources very thoroughly and done a great deal of thinking on the subject. His intention seems to have been to portray a most credible Saint, combining at the same time in one person as much of the available information as possible.

To some extent we are able to 'follow his tracks'.

He decided to reject the pagan myths. To the rationalist Snorri, a dyed-in-the-wool medieval Christian, it must have seemed inconceivable that a Christian king, a Saint even, could have believed in that kind of superstitious nonsense.

He was probably critical of the Church's exaggerated claims to miraculous cures and the like. In any case, he decided to use the legends of miracles sparingly, and to disperse them throughout his narrative (this in contrast to the arrangement in the Passio Olavi and the Saga of Legends).

As an aid to the listener/reader he composed a number of speeches, each one either giving the speaker's personality in capsule form — or providing a summing up of events. These speeches he put into the mouths of his historic characters. Scholars of our century have found, not surprisingly, that some of those speeches mirror the politics of his own time.

But, most important of all, Snorri portrayed the Saint as a person undergoing a perfectly logical human development: a mischievous and enterprising boy developing into an even more enterprising Viking chieftain, a converted king struggling to conquer his quick temper and tendency to cruelty, a man's saintliness painfully wrought by an effort of will — converting his grudging soul.

But even though Snorri's reseach was thorough and his intelligence keen, he lacked the means to break through the barrier of his sources, so as to discern, beyond them, the truth about the man Olav Haraldsson. What he did, was perfectly acceptable coming from an historian of his day — but the saga he produced, would, in our time, rather be termed an historical novel.

THE LEGACY OF SNORRI

Snorri was an author of unique gifts, and his picture of St Olav is highly convincing. So convincing, in fact, that until fairly recently no one questioned its authenticity. Even now his interpretation, or something closely akin to it, is taught in Norwegian schools.

But, one may ask, if his account is so excellent, why not settle for it and forget the rest?

For one reason: his portrait of the king is fiction, albeit excellent fiction; it is not history.

From the Snorri illustrations: St Olav's enemies gathering for battle at Stiklestad.

SNORRI AND HIS SOURCES

It would take us far afield, indeed, were we to examine here Snorri's St Olav saga, chapter by chapter, in order to determine how he employs his sources — also, it would hardly serve any useful purpose.

Instead, it should prove interesting to consider a couple of examples related to the material already dealt with.

One of these concerns a case of self-contradiction in connection with the battle of Stiklestad.

In his narrative of the battle, Snorri follows the Church's St Olav traditions, relating that the king refused to recruit into his army men who were not Christian. However, tucked away further back in his story, he quotes the following verse from Sigvat the Scald's great memorial poem to the king:

Some of the warriors believed
in God; the army was divided,
on his right hand the splendid one
arrayed those who were Christian.

This is the most important point, but not the only one, at which
Snorri gives two versions of the St Olav story: the official one
as proclaimed by the Church — and another tale clearly in
conflict with that. And his problem concerning conflicting
evidence seems obvious.

Sigvat had not been present at Stiklestad, but he knew the
story as told by those who had taken part in the battle. Snorri
must have known, as we know today, that the scald definitely
was not a man to eliminate the least particle of king Olav's
Christianity, if he could help it.

Consequently Snorri must have been torn between what he
considered a source not to be ignored — and his loyalty to the
Church. And he solved his dilemma by presenting both versions.

The other example concerns the pagan myth of Olav Geirstad-
alv and his sword. For the fact that Snorri left out the myth, did
not prevent him from mentioning the sword.

He refers to it when describing how the king was dressed and
armed for his final battle at Stiklestad; he points out: 'at his
belt he had the sword named Neite. That sword was extremely
keen, and golden threads were wound around its hilt.'

He seems to assume that 'the sword named Neite' is familiar
— without having as much as alluded to it up to that point.

Snorri also relates the conclusion of the story of the Saint and
his pagan sword — and here he is in agreement with older
sagas.

He recounts how king Olav went into battle carrying the
sword. And he relates that, after a while, the king was wounded
above his left knee. Reacting as a typical Viking, such a wound

should not have bothered Olav much, let alone have made him give up fighting — in another saga there is a story of a Viking who had both legs cut off in a battle, and who stood on the stumps shooting arrows from his bow — .

Instead, Olav, the Viking, does something that is unheard-of under such circumstances, and which his men must have experienced as an utter betrayal by their king. He leans on a rock, flings his sword far away, gives up the struggle — and turns to his God in prayer.

The sword king Olav throws away is that which, according to the myth, had been taken from Olav Geirstad-alv's burial mound and given to Olav as a child. However, since Snorri has not told the myth about that sword, the king's action loses much of its significance.

One may wonder whether the learned and thoroughly Christian Snorri, while discarding a myth he must have considered a superstition of ignorant people and unfit for his hero, in fact failed to grasp a problem that may have been vital to king Olav.

The Saint lived at a time when pagan beliefs were still very much alive in his country. To him the struggle between power represented by the God of Christianity and the power of pagan deities was undoubtedly very real. He had been brought up to believe himself the descendant of gods, most probably also to think himself the reincarnation of Olav the Geirstad-alv.

To someone possessing that kind of background, the sword Bæsing/Neite, taken from the Geirstad-alv's burial mound, may well have appeared as a token of his pagan right to be king — and its magic a promise of victory when he wielded it in battle. The sword may, in fact, have been the focal point of an inner struggle between the king's old faith not quite discarded, and his new faith not fully understood and integrated in his mind and heart.

If that was so — and I am certainly not declaring that it definitely was — , then Olav's throwing away of Olav Geirstad-alv's sword signified his ultimate conversion and his final surrender to the God of Christianity. Furthermore, in the eyes of the Church that one act could have vindicated him of his former violence and harshness — and justified bishop Grimkjell's act of canonizing the king.

Thus the rationalist Snorri may have missed one of the main points, possibly *the* main point, of his story.

The Saint and the God of Thunder

The pagan gods were vanquished, and their power was waning.

Tor, god of thunder and the protector of men against the destructive forces of nature — and the special foe of the dangerous giants, the trolls — had fought his last fight. Frøy and Frøya, god and godess of fertility, had lost their power — as had Odin, the many-faceted god of war and death, of magic and runic writing, wisdom, poetry and intoxicating drink.

But that did not happen overnight.

A PROCESS OF MORE THAN A HUNDRED YEARS

Christianity had been introduced to Norway before the birth of Olav Haraldsson. Norsemen travelled to foreign lands not only as marauders, but also as merchants, and some were converted — king Olav certainly was not the first man of power and influence to bring Christianity back to his native land.

Norway had had five Christian rulers before Olav Haraldsson. One was king Håkon, son of Harald Hårfagre, who tried to convert his countrymen, but in the end had to give up — he is the king mentioned above, who lacked wealth and therefore had to rely on the good-will of the aristocracy. Others were Harald Blåtann ('Bluetooth'), king of Denmark and of a part of Southern Norway, Olav Tryggvason, a descendant of Harald Hårfagre and king of Norway during the period 995—1000, and the earls Eirik and Svein of the Lade clan, who, according to the sagas, ruled Norway as vassals to the kings of Denmark and Sweden between the years 1000 and 1016, when Olav Haraldsson won his decisive victory.

The battle of Stiklestad was the main event, but still only one of many, in a development that continued for a long time. Scaldic lays indicate that in the 1050'ies king Olav's half-brother, Harald Hardråde ('the harsh ruler', Harald was king of Norway during the period 1046—1066) was still inflicting punishment on obdurate pagans in central districts of Southern Norway.

DEITIES IN HIDING

But what became of the pagan deities when the last pagan was converted, with or against his will? Were they forgotten entirely?

Most certainly they were not — they continued to inspire popular belief. In some places the female deities of fate, the 'norner', were remembered, in connection with childbirth, well into the nineteenth century: a special porridge served at the celebration of that event was called 'nornegrøt' ('grøt' meaning porridge). And I know a valley where a male doll was called a 'Tor' later than that — some vague reminiscence of idols representing that god must somehow have survived.

But, rather ironically, the pagan gods' best means of survival was to adopt various disguises. In the world of fairy-tales the red-bearded, hammer-wielding Tor, who had been a popular god indeed, appeared under the guise of a red-bearded, axe-carrying St Olav — and naturally, as part of it, was given a Christian veneer.

ST OLAV, TOR — AND THE SAGAS

The Saga of Legends contains a story which Snorri adopted in his saga, lock, stock and barrel (from the former saga, from Styrmir's version or from a source possibly common to the three of them). The subject is some of king Olav's problems during his flight from Norway to Sweden in the year 1028, and the miracles he performed in that connection. The place is Valldalen in the Western Norwegian district of Sunnmøre.

66

Like the pagan god Tor, the Saint was supposed to be a terror to trolls – here he transforms some into stone. Mural in Dingtuna Church, Västmanland, Sweden. From the period 1450–1520.

The story runs:

The farmer on the farm Muri was named Bruse; he was spokesman for the men of that valley. He and many others came to meet king Olav, and they received him well.

The king then asked if it were possible to go inland from that valley and on to Lesja (a community in the central part of Southern Norway).

Bruse replied that (further up) in the valley there was an immense scree (i.e. a great number of rocks that had fallen from its steep mountain sides). 'And no one, neither man nor horse, can get past it.'

King Olav said: 'We will have to try anyhow, farmer. And God's will shall prevail. You people bring your horses here in the morning, and we shall see what happens when we reach that scree, if we can find a way to cross, horses as well as men.'

Next morning the farmers came, as the king had told them, and they brought their horses. The horses moved goods and clothing, and the people, even the king, went on foot. He walked as far as the place named Krossbrekka ('the steep hill of the crosses'), at the top of which he rested. Taking in the view of the fjord below him, he said:

'My trusted men, those who have now shifted their loyalty, have given me a strenuous road to go. Yet, for a while they were my true friends.'

On the spot where the king sat, two crosses are now standing.

The king then mounted one of the horses, rode up through the valley and did not stop until he reached the scree.

He then asked Bruse if there was a summer farm where they could stay. Bruse said there was one. But instead the king pitched his tent and slept in that.

In the morning he told everybody to go to the scree and try if they could manage to get the packhorses through. They went, but the king stayed in his tent.

Towards evening they returned; the king's guardsmen as well as the farmers said they had worked hard without making any progress. And they said there would never be a road through that scree.

They stayed there another night, and the king prayed all night.

As soon as he saw the break of dawn, he told all his men to go to the scree and to try once more if they could manage to get the packhorses through. They went, but reluctantly, saying it would serve no purpose.

As soon as they were gone, the cook came to the king; he said that all the food they had left were two slaughtered sheep — 'and you have four hundred of your own men and a hundred farmers'.

The king told him to uncover all the cooking pots and put a little of the meat into each — and that was done. Then the king made the sign of the cross above the food and told the cook to prepare it.

The king went to the scree, where his men were trying to make a road. When he arrived, they were all sitting down, weary from the work.

Bruse said: 'I told you, lord, that this is impossible. But you would not believe me.'

The king then put his cloak down and told them all to go back and try once more.

This time twenty men were easily able to remove boulders that a hundred men had been unable to budge before. The road was ready by midday, and the people and packhorses could advance there as easily as if they were crossing a flat meadow.

After that the king went back to where the food was being cooked, the place that is now called Olavshelleren ('the cave of Olav'). There is a spring near that cave, and the king washed in it. In our time, if the cattle belonging to people of that valley are taken ill, they drink from the water of that spring and are cured.

Afterwards, the king and all the others ate. When the king had eaten his fill, he asked if there would be a summer farm in the valley beyond the scree, not too far from the mountain crossing — if so, they would sleep there that night.

Bruse said: 'There are some summer farms called Grønningene ('the green fields'), but no one can stay there at night because of the trolls and evil spirits that dwell in that place.'

The king said they should be on their way, and that he wished to spend the night at that summer farm.

Later the cook came and told him that they had plenty of food, 'and I do not know from where it came'.

The king thanked God for the good gift, and he let the people prepare bundles of food, for the farmers to bring along back to the valley.

As for himself, he stopped for the night at the summer farm.

In the middle of that night, when all were asleep, someone uttered a terrible scream outside, and a voice said: 'King Olav's prayers are burning me so badly that I have to leave my house. I flee now, and I shall never return to this summer farm.'

In the morning the king continued on his way across the mountains, but before he left, he said to Bruse:

'Build yourself a farm here, and the farmer in this place shall always make a livelihood. The grain shall never freeze on the farm, even if it freezes further down as well as further up the valley.'

The king then went on his way.

That tale is a composite made up of several elements.

The story of the food reminds one suspiciously of the Bible tale of Christ feeding more than five thousand people in 'a desert place'.

The feat of carving a road through an impossible scree, is one that Tor also accomplishes in another tale.

The chasing of the trolls is akin to a well known fairy tale (the impression of the fantastic is strengthened by the improbability of a summer farm being situated beyond an impassable scree), and also an exploit characteristic of Tor. St Olav is, incidentally, also known to have turned trolls, male and female, into stone. And his fame is not limited to Norway; a Swedish rhymed chronicle from approximately the time of the reformation (published in the year 1679), states:

> A troll that killed ten men,
> he turned into stone, still it stands.
> He chased other trolls away,
> now people are living in peace.

70

From the exiled catholic archbishop Olaus Magnus' book on the Nordic lands (published in Rome in the year 1555): Trolls that St Olav supposedly had transformed into stone, serving as landmarks along a pilgrim road from Sweden across the Dovre mountains to the Saint's shrine.

The story of the farm where the grain does not freeze, is an example of a common type of myth conceived to explain natural phenomena.

The healing spring is one of a great many that the Saint, according to traditions, made gush forth all over the country — even in places where he presumably never set foot. As a rule they are pagan sacred springs that have thus been christened.

ST OLAV IN LOCAL TRADITION

In addition to springs and petrified trolls, Saint Olav is supposed to have left various other kinds of landmarks, the lore of which is part of local tradition in many communities.

We shall use as our prime example a community which, according to the sagas, king Olav actually did visit: Lom in the district of Gudbrandsdalen in Southern Norway.

Snorri relates that the king, who had come across the mountains, reached a place with an excellent view of that community, which lies in a deep valley. The saga continues:

> 'It is a shame,' the king said, 'To burn a community as beatiful as this.'
>
> He and his men went down into the valley, to a farm named Nes (now: Synstnes, 'Southern Nes'). The king made his quarters there, and at the farm is a building where he slept; it is still standing and has not been changed since that time. The king stayed at Nes for five nights.

Snorri relates that king Olav sent a message to the farmers of Lom and of neighbouring communities; he gave them the choice between a battle with him and his men, in which case he promised to burn their farms — and baptism. Most of the farmers chose the latter; some, however, fled.

In the Lom of today a great many St Olav traditions have survived — even if people no longer take them literally.

There is a stone on which it is told that the Saint sat down to rest on his way from the mountains down into the valley. In two places there are tracks that his horse presumably left. There is a St Olav cave, a couple of St Olav springs, a huge footprint that he is supposed to have made, any number of stones that are in some way remarkable, for which he is given credit — and so on.

As for the house where he slept: the local museum has a St Olav building that has been moved there from the farm Synstnes. The Saint did certainly not sleep in the house as it exists today, but some of the logs from which it is built, seem ancient and may possibly have formed part of the famous house where he stayed — according to Snorri. Not quite in accord with the king's supposed saintliness is a local belief that his five nights at Nes had consequenses — some families in the vicinity have, at least until fairly recently, counted him among their forebears.

One does, in fact, find a mixture of fairy-tale elements,

probable remnants of pagan myths, and tales that, possibly, may contain a kernel of truth.

However, entirely belonging to the world of fairy tales is the story of the foot-prints that tradition in another place (Rauland in Telemark) claims to be those of the king and his men:

Totak (a large lake) is dangerous because of sudden squalls — even St Olav has been in danger there.

This happened one time when he wanted to cross the lake; he was halfway across when a storm broke. The winds were so fierce that the Saint had to admit he had never known worse weather.

But, by the aid of God, he and his men reached land; they jumped ashore on a point near the farm Haddeland, but their boat was crushed on the rocks. . . .

St Olav and his men stepped down so hard when they leaped ashore that their footprints still show — .

Those footprints, imbedded in the hard rock, are, in fact, part of a collection of rock carvings from the bronze age.

A Search for the Truth

I shall let our glimpse of the fairy-tale element complete this sojourn in the world of Saint Olav. We have come a long distance — from the scaldic poems praising king Olav's battles to the fabulous tales of a Saint identified with a god of thunder.

On the way we have, I believe, caught a few glimpses of how the human mind works — of how we are forever trying to clothe our ideals and/or idols in the dress we find most attractive.

The scalds emphasized their king's bravery and his good fortune in battle, which to them was a proof that he was favoured by the powers of fate.

The Church presented him as an ideal Christian ruler and a very effective example of piety and humility to his newly converted countrymen. The Saint's miracles were proclaimed with fervour in order to impress fully on people the power of God and his Saint.

The pagan myths gave glimpses of the world from which Olav Haraldsson emerged, a world in which he also was, in a way, a hero.

Then, in Snorri's rationalistic version of St Olav's saga, the portrait of the Saint was drawn to suit the preferences of a learned man of the thirteenth century, a man of refined taste and great understanding of the human condition.

Finally, in the fairy tales, people's fantasy was given full rein.

Around the year 1500: St Olav with his ax, his hanap, his dragon and in his armour. To his left another Norwegian Saint, Sunniva. She was killed when a cave collapsed, hence she carries a rock.

THE ELUSIVE SAINT

We have learned, through these tales, something about the needs, tastes and practical concerns of the people who told them.

But what, if anything, have we learned about Olav Haraldsson?

I have, personally, spent a great deal of time pondering the life and times of Saint Olav, and, for what they are worth, I have shared some of my thoughts with you.

But ultimately, I believe that Olav Haraldsson, Viking, king and Saint of the Church, will remain an enigma.

Events in the Life of St Olav

Saga dates that can not be substantiated from other sources, and therefore are considered doubtful, are given with a question mark.

A.D. 990?	Olav Haraldsson is born.
1002?	Olav leaves Norway in the hope of gaining fame and riches marauding in foreign lands.
1009	Olav and his Viking companions attack London and tear down London bridge.
1011	Olav takes part in the sack of Canterbury.
1013	(approximate date) Olav is baptised at Rouen.
1015	Olav returns to Norway. By an incredible stroke of luck he captures one of his most important enemies, earl Håkon of the Lade clan. He lets Håkon go, but extracts from him the promise that he will leave Norway and never meet Olav in battle.
1016	(Palm Sunday) Olav wins a decisive sea battle against earl Svein of the Lade clan and a great number of chieftains who owed their allegiance to the earl.
1016—1019?	Olav and the king of Sweden, incidentally his namesake, conduct a war of sorts, consisting of loud talk and border skirmishes.
1019?	Olav marries Astrid, daughter of the Swedish king, and the two kings make peace.
1024?	King Knut of Denmark and England demands of Olav that he become his vassal, which Olav indignantly refuses.

1026	Olav and his brother-in-law Anund, now king of Sweden, join forces against king Knut. A sea battle takes place at Helgeån (in present-day Southern Sweden) between, on one side, Olav and Anund, on the other side, Knut. Both parties claim victory.
1028	King Knut sails to Norway with a huge fleet and is proclaimed king of the land. Olav, who by this time has made himself extremely unpopular, is driven into exile by his own countrymen (December).
1029	King Knut goes back to England, leaving earl Håkon of Lade as his vassal. Olav leaves Sweden, where he has spent the winter, and goes to Russia.
1029 or -30	Earl Håkon drowns.
1030	Olav returns to Norway, where he is killed in the battle of Stiklestad on July 29th. Svein Alfivuson, king Knut's son, arrives in Norway to act as his father's vassal king.
1031	(August) Olav is canonized.

Sources and Literature

A bibliography including, in general, literature of relevance to our topic would be of a size entirely out of proportion to this small book. I shall therefore limit my list to literature quoted, referred to or used for reference in connection with the above. I shall, however, include a few bits of information that may be of use to the general reader.

Adam Bremensis, Gesta Hamburgensis ecclesiae pontificum, edited by B. Asmeidler *(Scriptores rerum Germanicum,* Hannover & Leipzig 1917), translated to English (Adam of Bremen: *History of the Archbishops of Hamburg—Bremen)* and edited by Francis J. Tschan (New York 1959).

Ágrip, (a short collection of sagas of the Norse kings) edited by V. Dahlerup (København 1880).

Ekre, Lars: *Stadnamn frå Midt-Jotunheimen* (Oslo 1960). This book, mainly concerning place names in central Southern Norway, also gives interesting information on local traditions.

Fagrskinna, edited by Finnur Jónsson (København 1902-03).

Faye, A.: *Norske Folke-Sagn* (Oslo 1948).

Flateyarbók, (mainly a collection of sagas of Norse kings, dating from around year 1400)), volumes I-III, edited by G. Vigfusson and C.R. Unger (Kristiania 1860-68).

Florence of Worcester, Chronicon ex Chronicis, edited by B. Thorpe (London 1848), translated to Danish and edited by Erling Albrechtsen (Odense 1982).

Gamal norsk homiliebok (including the older version of the Passio Olavi), edited by Gustav Indrebø, Oslo 1931.

Heimskringla (Snorri's sagas of Norse kings), edited by Bjarni Aðalbjarnarson and published as volumes XXVI-XXVIII in the series *Íslenzk fornrit* (Reykjavik 1979).

Historia Norvegiæ, (a short collection of sagas of Norse kings) edited by Gustav Storm *(Monumenta historia Norvegiæ,* Kristiania 1880), translated into Norwegian *(Norges historie)* by A. Salvesen (Oslo 1969).

Landstad, M.B.: *Mytiske sagn* (Oslo 1926).

Munch, P.A.: *Det norske folks historie,* (History of the Norwegian people), part 1, volume 2 (Christiania 1853).

Olafs saga hins helga (The Saga of Legends), edited by O.A. Johnsen (Kristiania 1922).

Otte Brudstykker af den ældste Saga om Olav den Hellige (eight fragments from the oldest St Olav saga), edited by G. Storm (Christiania 1893).

Passio et miracula Beati Olavi, edited by F. Metcalfe (Oxford 1881).

Saga Óláfs konungs hins helga (Snorri's great saga of St Olav, including interpolations from Styrmir's saga of the Saint), volumes 1-2, edited by O.A. Johnsen and J. Helgason (Oslo 1930-41).

St Olav — seine Zeit und sein Kult, (Acta Visbyensia VI, Visby 1981).

Sveaas Andersen, P.: *Samlingen av Norge og kristningen av landet 800—1130* (Bergen—Oslo—Tromsø 1977).

The Anglo-Saxon Chronicles, translated and collated by Anne Savage (London 1982).

Theodoricus monachus, Historia de antiquitate regum Norvegiensium, (a short collection of sagas of Norse kings) edited by Gustav Storm *(Monumenta historica Norvegiæ,* Kristiania 1880); translated into Norwegian *(Historien om de gamle norske kongene)* by A. Salvesen (Oslo 1969).